Pearl and Bone

'It is a celebration of the triumphs and strengths of women as well as sharing their vulnerabilities and sensitivities.'
– **Maddy Templeman,** *The Broken Spine*

'A captivating collection of poetry which flows between moments of tenderness and harrowing rawness.'
– **Billie Ingram-Sofokleous,** *Buzz Magazine*

'Her poems are full of fragility and vulnerability, but also strength and celebration, evoking the strange miracles of pregnancy and birth.'
– **Rachel Carney,** *Created to Read*

Praise for *Salacia:*

'These poems are visceral, inventive, with every riff packed to the brim with awe.'
– **Rhian Edwards**

'*Salacia* coaxes sublimity from pain, reminding us that though we may be hurt, we can still be powerful.' – **Zoë Brigley**

'Mari Ellis Dunning writes with honesty about mental disorder and the intricacies of depression, but her poetry is charged by the body and the senses.'
– **Anna Lewis**

'Mari Ellis Dunning brings to life a world in which Welsh women do not write their own stories, but rather have stories written upon them.'
– **Gareth Leaman,** *Poetry Wales*

'Cyfrol o gerddi sydd yn tywys y darllenydd drwy a thros foroedd o emosiynau – yn ddi-ofn, yn agos iawn at y pridd. [...] Nid mwynhau darllen cerddi Mari Ellis Dunning mae rhywun o reidrwydd ond neidio ar 'rollercoaster' yn y ffair a gwibio heibio merched ar grogbrennau.'

'A volume of poems that guide the reader through and over seas of emotions – fearless, cutting close to the bone. [...] Reading Mari Ellis Dunning's poems is like jumping on a rollercoaster at the fair, and whizzing past women at the gallows.' – **Rhys Mwyn, Radio Cymru**

Mari Ellis Dunning's first poetry collection *Salacia* was shortlisted for the Wales Book of the Year Award, and was followed by *The Wrong Side of the Looking Glass,* a pamphlet of dramatic monologues written in collaboration with Natalie Ann Holborow. She won the Terry Hetherington Young Writers Award and placed second in both the Lucent Dreaming Short Story Competition and the Sylvia Plath Poetry Prize. A PhD candidate at Aberystwyth University working on a historical novel exploring accusations of witchcraft and fertility, Dunning also teaches creative writing part time. She lives on the west coast of Wales, in Llanon, with her husband, their two sons and their dog.

mariellisdunning.cymru

Pearl and Bone

Mari Ellis Dunning

Parthian, Cardigan SA43 1ED
www.parthianbooks.com
First published in 2022
© Mari Ellis Dunning 2022
ISBN 978-1-913640-72-9
Editor: Susie Wildsmith
Cover image: 'Christine Keeler Mesmerises' by Fionn Wilson
Cover design by Syncopated Pandemonium
Typeset by Elaine Sharples
Printed and bound by 4edge Limited, UK
Published with the financial support of the Welsh Books Council
British Library Cataloguing in Publication Data
A cataloguing record for this book is available from the British Library

Pearl and Bone is provided to selected libraries across Wales with support of The Borzello
Trust to promote the reading of contemporary poetry by new and emerging voices.

annwyl Llew, fy nghalon

Nobody has ever measured, not even poets,
how much the heart can hold.
– Zelda Fitzgerald

CONTENTS

Foreword

When I first saw those two pink lines appearing, like small fish rising to the surface of a pond, there was no way of knowing I would be undergoing half my pregnancy, the entirety of my labour and the majority of the first year of my son's life under strict lockdown conditions. The range of emotions and new experiences brought about by becoming a mother for the first time, compounded with it happening during a global pandemic, pulled poetry from me like water from a tap. It also led me to reflect on how sidelined and marginalised new parents, particularly women and mothers, were in amongst the full scale of the pandemic. I spent seemingly endless hours labouring alone, then spent a week on the postnatal ward while my premature baby strengthened in SCBU, with no physical support from family, friends or even my husband. Meanwhile, friends sent selfies from the pub. This marginalisation didn't feel like an isolated incident – at best, we were overlooked. At worst, the situation showed total distain and misogyny from the government and policy makers, who consistently prioritised retail and 'the economy' over the health and wellbeing of thousands of new parents. Forming the vast majority of primary caregivers, women and mothers bore the brunt of this dismissal.

Despite being necessary, vital and gruelling, the greater part of care work, largely considered 'women's work', remains unseen, unrecognised and devalued. Studies indicate that stay-at-home mothers work, on average, the equivalent of 2.5 full time jobs, and yet these hours are generally unacknowledged by policy makers, society at large, and women themselves. My sudden immersion into this world – that of a full-time caregiver in the middle of a pandemic when baby groups, cafes and libraries were firmly closed – led me to consider the rights of women globally, particularly in regards to reproductive rights. As I looked more closely, I was startled, but not surprised, by the violence and vitriol surrounding the issue of female bodily autonomy.

We are living in a time in which a presidential candidate brazenly bragged about sexually assaulting women and was still elected. He then proudly posed for a photo depicting himself signing away women's rights to their own bodies, stripping funding for sex education and access to safe, legal abortion. Since its introduction in 1984, The Global Gag Rule has put millions of women's lives at risk, particularly poorer women, and counterintuitively resulted in higher rates of accidental pregnancy and an increase in dangerous and deadly abortion procedures.

At the time, the impact of this withdrawal of funding under America's anti-abortion rhetoric had far-reaching consequences beyond restricting reproductive rights, impacting on contraceptive services, antenatal care, HIV testing and treatment, and screening for cervical, breast and prostate cancer across Kenya, Nepal, Nigeria and South Africa.

In her essay, 'A Nation Divided on Abortion', Zoë Brigley described the 2020 presidential race as a 'referendum on abortion'. That The Global Gag Rule ultimately increases the number of abortions by reducing access to contraception is not just an unfortunate irony – it reveals the way in which women's bodies repeatedly become political spaces used to control and coerce.

In spring 2022, just before going to print with this collection, a leaked Supreme Court draft opinion suggested the court could be poised to overturn the historic Roe v. Wade ruling, leaving the legal status of abortion entirely up to individual states, again compromising millions of women's lives in a bid to control and claim ownership of all female bodies.

With this in mind, I wrote many of the poems included within this collection, including the final poem 'The Womb Speaks', which speaks back to The Global Gag Rule, and to the fear surrounding an empty womb. What is it about women's bodies that drives the state to repress, control and undermine our choices? Is it the power we hold as women and child-bearing people to create, grow and nourish new life? To sustain a collection of cells from conception to birth? Does the ability to occupy the space between life and death, the almost supernatural magic of pregnancy and birth, ignite fear in some government officials and heads of state? Enough fear to repeatedly strip us of our rights to our bodily autonomy?

In November 2019, an Ohio bill ordered medical practitioners to re-implant ectopic embryos into a woman's uterus or face charges of 'abortion murder', despite the procedure being physiologically impossible. In the same year, an Alabama woman, Marshae Jones, was indicted for manslaughter after losing a pregnancy having been shot in the abdomen, while her shooter remained free. She was charged on the grounds of having 'provoked' the attacker. Similarly, in El Salvador, women who suffer the tragedy of miscarriage and stillbirth still face prison sentences on charges of murder.

Most people would say we've come a long way since the infamous witch trials of the 16th century, and while we don't typically hang women in market squares or burn them at the stake on unfounded charges anymore, many of the same issues of fear and control abound today. A 2022 study by the Global Institute for Women's Leadership found that one in three men across thirty countries believe feminism does 'more harm than good.' America has yet to see a female president – indeed, during Hilary Clinton's campaign she was repeatedly referred to as 'The Wicked Witch of the Left' – the gender pay gap remains unresolved, and bias against women in medicine is rife. How much has really changed, in terms of attitude, since Heinrich Kramer launched a violent attack on women, claiming in the Malleus Maleficarum 'when a woman thinks alone, she thinks evil?' What he, and other witch finders, seemed to fear most, was the notion of a powerful, independent woman. Can we really suggest anything has changed in regards to cultural attitudes towards women, particularly in regard to law-makers, heads of state and religion?

Most people will be aware of Monica Lewinsky, a twenty-four-year-old White House secretary who was vilified following an affair with then-president Bill Clinton, who quickly reduced her to no more than 'that woman' in his infamous speech. While Clinton will be remembered for numerous events, Lewinsky's name will always be synonymous with the affair. Her story mirrors, to some extent, the woman at the heart of the Profumo affair, a major scandal in 20th-century British politics. Her name was Christine Keeler, and I am grateful to Fionn Wilson for granting me permission to use her painting of Keeler on the cover of this book. Keeler was just nineteen when she embarked on an affair with John Profumo, the Secretary of State for War in Harold Macmillan's Conservative government. In a pattern we have seen time and again, Keeler, having been essentially groomed and manipulated by some of the most powerful men in the world, was publicly shamed, mocked and ridiculed. I am fascinated by Keeler, by the public's treatment of her, particularly as she aged, and by the lack of any conceivable change in cultural attitude even sixty years later. A series of poems in this collection are dedicated to Christine Keeler, her story interweaving with my own. She is emblematic of the women world-over who have unduly suffered due to the media, the state, the government, public perception and cultural attitudes.

These issues – of medical bias, gendered violence, misogyny, control over women's bodies and reproductive rights, the praising of chastity and virginity, and the notion of female bodies as vessels alone – are far too much for a foreword in a poetry collection to tackle, and too vast an issue to explore through poetry alone, but this collection, *Pearl and Bone,* is my starting point.

Mari Ellis Dunning
2022

It is slavery: the claim to own and control another's body, and to profit by that claim.
– Margaret Atwood

Telling your father at Bwlch Nant yr Arian

We're going to have a baby,
I told your father, just days since I'd felt his ribs slot
like coins between mine.
We were toeing a mountain trail, me dancing
towards the edges, him gripping
the cliff face like a scattering fern.
He stopped, looked out at the scoop of valley,
the way it sung beneath us, the silver
brook steaming like an umbilical cord, said: *no,*
it's too soon to tell.

I'm not sure he believed in your existence
until you were hooked, solid and squirming,
in his quivering arms.

You were a fish

                    fidgeting
in my belly, the day we watched
your father straddling a paddleboard,
riding the horizon like a chariot
coursing the sun, the dog darting
up and down
the jetty, sea-bass slick.
We counted each stroke
of his oar slicing the water.

In the thick heat you whorled, flipped,
kicked your own rhythm
against my midriff, spun
small waves inside
until I thought I could see you,
your mackerel-small gleam,
spinning on the sea
            with your father,
            rolling like a pearl.

A body changing

By four months my body relinquished itself,
underwear scoring my hips like wires,
tracing seams on my skin,
fleshing out a brand new hemline.

A new mould

There was no grinding,
no   seismic shift   as my hip
   bones   shoved   outwards.
Only   a slow,   silent   stretching,
my   edges   moulding
the shape
       of a mother.

Flash

(Christine Keeler astride an Arne Jacobsen chair, 1963)

A sunless studio in Soho. Smoke curling
                    the stairwell. Trumpet creeping like vines
from the ground floor. *Flash*. I did as I was told.

Stood stripped and bare as a newborn foal. Straddled
                    the chair. Leant into its unyielding grain.
Fizzed at its rigid geometry. The way it cinched the waist,

shielding the softest parts of me. The powdery folds
                    of my belly. Glared at the camera lens like a lover.
Unabashed. In twenty-nine frames he captured every

fragment – my upper lip bowed like a harp. The small crease
                    between my eyebrows like the pleat of a sheet.
Defiant wrinkle pressed to my nose. Later,

they listed all the men I'd taken to bed. Asked,
                    are there any you actually loved?

                              Are there any who loved you?

Lewis Morley: Christine Keeler, 'The Chair,' 1963

Page of Wands

So this is who he'll be –
standing centre stage
flushing apricot and gold.
Commanding the skies.

When he tells the barren land
to bloom, it will listen.

There is a reason he perched
at the very top of the deck, leapt
like a hare to meet you.
        He is within you.

See how he presses
his scroll to chest,
how leaves sprout from his staff
like poetry. Like song.

He will pluck words from you
like daffodils from the earth.

Just wait: he will set
your world on fire.

On finding a spider under the sink

You were only weeks away when I started to soak
rags, froth water over the tiles, and scrub
the months away in hardened globs of coffee.

When countertops glinted like new moons
I found her: a trapeze artist swinging
at the underside of the sink, eight legs resting

on silk spun silver as tin, her clutter
of babies sandgrain-small. Still. Dreaming
of days to come, picturing their lives beyond
the easy warmth of the kitchen cupboard.

Xenomorph

She stalks her way through vents,
all stealth tactics and screaming girders,

She's a woman of few words, creaking
shingles. She'll rip you clean

in two, plunge innards with a tail
dense as bone, bludgeon limbs

with thwacking ease. She scuttles
in air ducts, clunks her jaws on skullcaps,

plummets Nostromo's bowels,
doesn't kill the cat. She jumps ship.

She thrusts and thrusts.

Mary

Mary paces the stable, heels trailing
straw, belly timbrel-round. Joseph grapples
limply at her palms, cups water to her lips,
kneads her shoulders with aching hands.
All night, he has rapped his knuckles at stubborn
doors, the donkey trampling earth at his ankles.
They have listened to the echo again and again:
there are no lodgings here. And so he watches the child
crowning in the hay, kicks dirt under his feet
while they wait. She has told him the baby
is a miracle, a golden gift conceived
in a thundering of wings, a crushing light.
Now stretching her taut as a bowstring,
now mewling beneath the stars.

Mary Magdalene

Despite what they say, I never bowed
to smooth his feet with suds, never stooped
at his calloused toes. For years,
we walked hand in hand, shaking sand loose
from our shoulders, commanding miracles
of fish scales and wheat, insisting the ground
rise beneath our feet. If I knelt,
it was at his side. Before they made a cross
of his tired body, and strung a sickening halo
of thorns at his temple, I pressed my lips
to his. Left an ocean of salt at his cheekbones.
Swore to keep his name, like honey,
on my tongue. When they threw him, tanned
as a nut, to the dust, only then did I fold in two.

Eve

When Adam grew bored
of plucking heads from daisies,
God pulled me from his side,
　　whittled my waist
　　from a glinting rib,
said, *this should keep you busy.*

It's true, our garden was plum-ripe,
lush as a sprawling wreath,
rose-flecked, ocean vast,
but women can grow weary, too.

I liked the small serpentine
　　thrill, slithering long
and loose as a constellation of pearls,
the way he branched his body
like velvet rope, his fig-sweet breath,
his voice of spiced honey. I liked
the glorious threat of fangs.

　　Try the fruit, he said, coiling,
　　languid, at the tree's ridged spine.

The apple was a blood moon
in my palm, a garnet scrabbled like a bulb
from the earth. Its juice seeped
sweet from my lips, rolled
a reckoning over my chin.
A thunderbolt struck the sky.

When God exiled us, clattering
the gates to a deafening close,
Adam fumbled for my fist,
whimpered like a hound at my side,
coupled his palms, and I

                       took

                            another

                                 bite.

July 2nd, 15:08

All morning, you were an acrobat, barreling
headfirst, feet to the milky way, elbowing
through the darkness. For hours, your burnished
taproot sluiced my core. You steamed ahead, little
adventurer, blazing like the sun. By afternoon,
you were an eel, slipping from between my thighs,
grey and barely breathing. A bloodied sigh. Then,
that newborn mewl, hooking through the stillness,
a cacophony of cries, the thundering beauty of lungs.

Current

His birth stirs a current
    in me,   calls forward
        an ocean,
makes a tidal wave of my core.
        I let the swell carry
           me like debris
              until he gushes

                loose,

  a furious
     limpet thrust
       earthside
          in water and salt.

Sickness   and heat.

  We beg him:
      breathe—

           Wait.

    A new continent takes shape.

A Sudden Mother

(Staying on the postnatal ward during Covid-19)

There is no sleep here, where women shuffle, barefoot.
Elasticated waistbands. Nightgowns trailing linoleum.
We are pale and bloodless ghosts. We are waning
moons. We do not speak to one another. In a bed
feet from mine, someone chokes, a sob thick as toffee
cloying her throat. An indifferent curtain hangs between us.
Somewhere on the ward, a baby cries, pitching its vowels
to the ceiling fan. The baby isn't mine. My baby is a lost
creature, hibernating in a sterile incubator, a corridor stretching
between us like a deep lake. Tubes like terrible worms
curling his nostrils. Burrowing into his hands. He has shaken
something loose in me, like coins rattling in an old tin. I swell
and I leak. A sudden mother. For a week, it goes like this:
me, wringing my hands at his cribside, my stupid pupils dry
and wide. Watching his heartbeat form steady mountaintops
against the darkness. Friends framed like portraits,
stuttering their congratulations through phone screens.
His father, pitched miles away, butting at doors that scream:
Stop.
No entry.

Peter

(Christine Keeler gives birth)

Sweet sixteen and forced to pace the bedroom
like a lynx, curtains drawn shut as eyelids, my torso
rounding like a watermelon, the spinal ache, and now
the neighbours really will have something to talk about.

I coaxed a pen firm inside, tried to scribble him away
in ink, magpie-black, spent evenings in a fug of
                    castor oil, gin, whisky
drew baths so hot I scalded my thighs pink as piglets,
felt the breath seep slow from my lungs,

while still his wretched heart beat   and beat   and beat
and *push in a knitting needle – that's what works best,* they said.

Still, he fought his way out, barrelled into this world bruised
and unwanted as a curse, *a half-dead bawling infant,*
until they parcelled his writhing fists and bloodied knees,
            carted him away like a soiled bedsheet.

Preterm

for four weeks
you slept

a lost thing
clinging to me

your legs drawn
like a frog

not yet ready
to leap

you were *preterm*
clamped

at my chest
still striving for darkness

not yet ready
for the world

                                        part of it
                                        nonetheless

Spell for a Mother

When he arrives,
become a noctambulist.

Pace the bedroom
with him clutched

to your chest. Befriend
the moon. Watch

her wax nightly. See her
silver light glimmer

like web-silk over
his spine. After all,

isn't this what you
longed for?

This translucent
creature bellowing

into the night. Refusing
sleep. The way he scrambles

at your breasts for hours,
suckling and screaming.

Relinquish yourself
to this broadside assault

of the senses, the swelling
and throbbing at your

temples, stomach, labia.
Plead with him again.

Each morning, scrape
the pepper corns of sleep

from your eyes. Forget
to butter your toast. Slink

from room to room, shuffling
between kitchen cabinet

and coffee table, your dead
weight making a bog

of the carpet. Keep him
strapped to your torso

like a fleshy bomb.
Marvel at his peachy

skin, the golden warmth
of it. Wrinkle your nose

at the crown of his head
and know: *he is yours.*

On Walking in the Rain

When you came, I stopped
minding the rain, learned to enjoy

its cool touch like freshly
laundered sheets on my cheek.

We trailed endless miles, you
bound to my chest, a chimp

flexing your fist, one arm tumbling
loose. The dog strapped to my wrist.

What else was there to do
in a world licked clean by salt

and wind, shut
as a stubborn mouth.

When you came, I saw the rain
for what it was – a thousand small

kisses at my temple. A baptism
amongst the slangs.

Sometimes we sit in the car

Mid-afternoon and you have finally slackened,
folded into your carseat like a dormouse, a tightly
strapped parcel going nowhere. My hands flounder,
useless, grip the steering wheel for something to do.
Rain pelts us like gunfire. Your breath
comes soft as blanket folds. I don't know
why my hands are shaking.

Lovesick

'Just a mixed up

        love sick

           young girl

that long

        hot summer

when the temperatures   soared

           nuclear as missiles.'

Escape

'From the very first moment
the press started baying
at Wimpole Mews, rounding
like a pack of hyenas,
bloodthirsty and frothing
for pillow-pressed secrets
and the curve of my hips,
there was no escape
from being Christine Keeler.'

Daffodils

The daffodils are back
again, pushing up like sunbeams.
It's been a year since their last
hesitant peek and I am unrecognisable
in my nightdress, an infant clamped
to my waist. The seasons have passed
in silence – a summer of rounding
like a blueberry, my baby curled
safe inside; the stumble that broke
the sack, thrust him, unexpected,
into the world. Through autumn
we paced the living room, lapping
   sofa, armchair, bookcase
again and again. Relearned faces
in two dimensions. In winter
the garden stiffened and cracked,
and still it was just the two of us,
learning side by side
and waiting for the daffodils
to surface again.

Oviraptorosaurs, unhatched

For sixty-six million years you've waited, curved
like a crustacean, spine forming a perfect arch,
tight as a clenched fist. Each ridge a bone white
knuckle. You are tucked in anticipation, stone-hardened,
impatient for the hatching. You long for the feathers
that will not sprout. The wings that will not grow.

Poem for Marshae Jones

The next thing she knows,
she is a waning moon,
stomach flattening to a pinch,
scarlet draining between her thighs.
Maybe I provoked her, she thinks,
as her thumbs are pressed to ink.
Smeared black mitosis. The steel
door clangs shut as a fist, someone
else's sobs roll through her cell,
siren-loud, new-born blue,
reckless as a clamouring
       of bullets.

Poem for Sarah Everard

Tonight, she is not afraid to walk
these streets alone, knows their contours

like the valleys of her own body. Alleys
and gulleys familiar as old lovers.

The lights hook her cheekbones.
        Stars sputter.

He approaches, palms outstretched,
vowing only to serve. To protect.

So this. This is how it ends,
        her bones split to dust,

ground like a beetle to the earth.
Voice wilting in his grip.

She cannot know how her name
will echo in the mouths of strangers.

How it will grow, like a daisy,
clawing back, relentless, through the soil.

A woman born of flame

After Christina Thatcher

How she slid earthside in sweat and heat,
her mother crouched at the belly bite, fire
wringing smoke at her temples. How she carried
the heat with her, always – tending fever,
endless bodies hot and writhing on sick beds.
Flinging boiled water, a scorching baptism.
How she cracked skies with thunder,
parted clouds, electric as a goddess.
Formed rubies in the earth like bloodstones.
How she felt the heat of shame on her cheek,
ripe as a lashing. The burn of rope, a coiled
snake about her wrists. How she ended
it all in ash and dirt. Licked sterile with flame.

The first year

1.

We've circled the sun, lapping planets
in a dog-tired haze. For a year,
you've slept at my collarbone, spent days
perched on this new curve of hip,
inquisitive as a jackdaw, pressed
your hot little cheek to mine.
Blindly, we've stumbled the slangs,
mapped our own trail through the mud,
learning together what it is
         to be
               this.

2.

Since you arrived, we've left behind
     Mars
         Jupiter
             Saturn
watched countless stars die.
I am still learning
to be your mother, and already,
you have learned
     to carry yourself.

the house changed too

by now there are traces / of you / in every room /
each corner / a spluttered clash of colour / hand
puppets / carpet the living room / like carcasses /
lions / and tigers / and frogs / oh my / and your highchair
scuffing the wall / barricaded / to stop you mounting /
its summit / come crashing / down / with a clatter / palm prints
pressed to glass / your ghostly fingertips already /
outgrown / half a dozen / nappies / hanging limp
as dead turkeys / from the washing line / socks
breadcrumb a trail / leading me / always / back / to you

Letter from Zelda Fitzgerald

You've fallen for a whirlwind, no net
strong enough to quell, but
you are the only person on earth
who ever loved all of me. You had me
       parcelled and delivered
to wear like a watch-charm at your sleeve,
or a buttonhole pinned near your heart.
Darling, I will sprawl my petals
               at your heels.

I'm so glad you came, like summer,
when I needed you most. Everything seems
so smooth and restful now, like this yellow
dusk, and every day I love you more, but
       I am losing all pretence of femininity
and I know I would aggravate you to death
today. If only I could stop reading *Scott*
in every line. Stop seeing your face
in every shadow and flame.

       Now all these soft, warm nights
will go to waste when I ought to be dying
in your arms under the moon. Old death
is so very beautiful.
       We will die together, my love—   I know.

Poem for Bertha Mason

They say I scuttle like a beetle,
belly low, dragging filth
at my heels. Hear them whisper
about the maniac, that woman crouched
in the corner, pissing on the floorboards
like a pitbull. They say I will tear
                the meat
    from your bones
          while you sleep.

When he brought her home to Thornfield
I scoured her face for my own, crept
nightly through her room, marvelled
at her skin, stark as a milky eye. I dreamed
of fire. Of flames kissing their cheekbones.

Before the wedding, her veil hung limp
as a dead swan from my scalp. I tore it
clean in two. They said it was madness.
They said I was Rochester's curse, but *reader,*
    I married him first.

Acknowledge me: I am more than a metaphor.
A charcoal-haired symbol, howling like a beast.
A plot device steaming ash and smoke.
These rotting floorboards rock like waves,
the window lunges open, like a woman finally
speaking, like arms outstretched. A welcome home.

The Moon

Countless as stars, they've mined my shadows
for that illusive shimmer, laid claim to my brow
in reckless bounds. Boots trampling the chalky
pallor of my cheeks, like cigarette stubs
   burning through carpet.

Still, I have only ever remained silent. Waited.
Watched with my doe-black eyes,
my pockmarked chin, for a misplaced step,
     a loose shard,
the sudden spinning-top of a man lost to darkness.

They say I should be grateful, to have my bones
dusted and scaled, to be photographed, adored
as a gleaming starlet, but I am tired
of their unrelenting leaping, their one small step
for man, their space race propaganda.

The way they pocket parts of me, like rubies,
  to carry home.

Song for a Bird's Skull

I find it peeking through a thicket-snare,
glistening opaline-white in the brambles. Cradle
it, cup it in my palm like a precious thing, cap arched
bald and stark as a stone; this slight scalp, smooth
as fingernails, its beak still hooking birdsong.
Threads of bone woven like silk. I press
it to the curve of my ear like a seashell, listen
for the prehistoric bleat of the forest. This small,
translucent husk, with its eggshell ridges, spills
the chirruping of every wagging blade of grass,
every shuck of riverbed, the soft mulch
and sigh of autumn. The slow chords of songs
gathered like pearls, held, still, inside the marrow.

Woman and Child, Qinghai

What we know is this: the earth
shook like an excavated root, loosed
mud thick enough to bury them
where they knelt. See the ferocity
in her grip. She is buckled at the knees
and steadfast as a bulwark as she clasps
the child to her chest like a newborn.
Petitions the skies. For four thousand
years, her arms have been a barricade
about his shoulders. Her heart,
      his resting place.

Christine Keeler meets Romeo

She drapes herself over the balcony,
a languid cat in summer heat, offers
the branches a glimpse of thigh, a sliver
of freshly powdered collar bone. Calls out:
  Romeo, Stephen, John, Lucky.
Romeo presses himself to the thickets,
gathers roses to his chest, says, *she speaks,*
but she says nothing. He is not listening,
sees only the silhouette of her robe,
the velvet and milk of her skin. The night
clings to her, tacky and hot as suede.
A glance at her oil-slathered bust,
and Romeo saunters home, satisfied,
spitting her name. Her face already forgotten.

Poem for Christine Keeler

In the docks I stood flushed, the truth
      stripped from my back
like a torn dress, fragments caught
in the mouths of strangers. Stephen
holding my gaze – *chin up, little baby.*
For two hours and thirty-eight minutes
they hounded, flayed my skin
like apple peel, sluiced me to my core
      until the gavel beat
down a bellowing heart, singing
out its verdict: *guilty.* Tell me,
am I still your little baby? Your doe-eyed
seductress, the showgirl kitten-licking
your bruises. Your dead-eyed siren.
      More dangerous than Russia.

Poem for Mary Wollstonecraft

She wanes. My little sparrow, paling
like a tired moon in my arms.
Pressed to my breast she refuses
to drink, her tongue coiling
obscene angles, lips smacking
powder-dry.

The days pass by in sweat
and heat. Sickness and sourness
furring my tongue. Fever dreams
broken only by her chirruping
until
      she is   torn
                    away. My milk
now yellowed and curdling.

They tell me she is learning to wear
her own skin, familiar as a blanket,
that she waxes, growing fat and soft
as cream. I picture her, my baby
girl, rounding like an apple
at someone else's chest.

Idle pansies bob at my bedside.
Wine sweetens my lips. Before I leave,
they christen her Mary, let her carry
my name in the swell of her cries.
I wonder if she feels me in her bones,
if her heart beats in time with mine.

This Thing with Teeth

Is this what mother's love is like –
this thing with teeth that dwells
in me, this feral she-wolf
tending her wounds? I have
become a lighthouse watching
the tide, a heron circling the water's
edge, a red dwarf, unseen.

A body, postpartum

I am learning,
        now, to recognise
someone new, to meet her
in the mirror and say: *this.*
This is where he grew, like a fledging
rolling cartwheels day and night.

This pocket of flesh you turn
from, his first home. These doorframe
hips his foundations. Beneath
your waistband he learned your voice,
spent months conjuring your face
in his dreams.

This is where his limbs stretched
like oars, where he paddled
the darkness. In the pleats
of these scars he felt your love
streaming, rich and hot along
the umbilicus.

When she glares from the glass,
I am learning to welcome her,
like an old friend, changed.

Blessing for the Lost Ones

In a matter of weeks, you make tombs
of their bodies, encase yourselves in capillaries
and flesh then dull your hearts to a quiet stop.
You strip the sickness from them, laying still
and warm as unshelled prawns. Wait to be uncovered
in a monochrome haze, laying lifeless beneath
the probe. Holding on just long enough for your
mothers to catch a glimpse of your form, a small
white jelly bean hovering on screen. Knowing
this is what she needed, before she could let
you go. Before you could finally leave her.

Blessing for the Women

i.m. Roe v. Wade

i.

a thin pink line that sealed
　your fate in seconds, left you heaving
on the carpet, knowing he had violated
you twice over: once in the car park
　under a flickering neon light,
and again now, leaving a trace
　of himself inside you, to grow
slow, like a tumour you might
　　　learn to love

ii.

you were too young even to realise
　the bleeding had stopped, it wasn't coming
monthly yet anyway. By the time you were
certain, your middle was already watermelon
　round, the whispers audible behind the hands
of strangers. A child carrying
　　a child of her own

iii.

you longed for that baby. Had told the world,
　sharing names and nursery ideals: rainbows
　and rocking horses clouding your vision.
It wasn't until you laid down for the sonographer,
bare bellied as a salmon, that you saw the small bulge

in your fallopian tube, learned the awful truth –
   the child would never have survived,
       but you still could

   iv.

the night was dense with oud
  and rose oil, as you moved together,
  packing your nails with dirt
  and his skin cells, listening
to the tawnies calling into the night.
  The length of his body like cooling
rope against yours, the glug and beat
of your hearts as one. The torn
  latex no more than an overlooked
     mistake

   v.

your breath came syrup-thick, fast
  as a wild horse galloping, the tremble
and sob at your core, the realisation
that your body was now your own
     personal prison cell,
     governed by men
     you had never even met.

Altar

There wasn't a lot of choice, but there was some, and this is what I chose,
– Margaret Atwood, *The Handmaid's Tale*

So this is where you worship:
      at the tired altar of your own shame,
knees pressed to marble. You have stiffened
      here for years now, waiting
for your own forgiveness, but still, they pile
      in, these thoughts nudging
and shoving like a congregation, bellowing
      about the way his stomach felt
when pinned against yours. *Did you say no?*
      In quick vocals they remind you of the warm,
unwelcome fug of his tongue on the roof
      of your mouth, *no,* the fungus-creep of his hair
shedding over your skin. They ask again:
      did you ever say no? They kneel beside you.
Bleating that, despite what you said, it was you
      that first laid in the bed.

Knotweed

it settles like knotweed in the stomach
this quiet, unknowable thing,
these spiralling green tendrils,
this ever-growing ache.

Former Showgirl Unrecognisable
(Christine Keeler ages)

Decades later, the papers printed my face, spun
headlines from my name: K E E L E R. They were crows
chattering, jabbing their beaks at every ruck
and fold, shaping a circus of the skin gathered
like cloth at my elbows. My paperbag knees a parade –
Former showgirl unrecognisable. I am the hourglass
that bloated and cracked, spilling sand and scandal.
The swollen woman tugging her trolley with a fist
once filled with secrets. Profumo's trace sits deep
in the creases of these palms, still. If only they knew
they were right all along: Yes, I was *Mother. Whore. Hag.*
I was just a pretty nobody. I was capable of cutting down kings.

Leaving

i.
After I left, I dreamt of climbing,
        the mounting impossibility
of navigating the ascent   alone,
        with pram wheels jutting
at awkward angles,
        like a cage of splintered ribs.

ii.
In the bag: a heap of white vests,
        like clean sheets of paper;
a wooden rattle, clamouring;
        a mound of balled
socks to keep the baby's toes bundled,
        warm as a rabbit's.

iii.
We trundled miles and miles,
        the motorway stretching
a steel grey ocean.
        In time, he will learn –
even a queen will leave
        her hive when the honey sours.

Spilled Milk

For a year you guzzled, slurped
nourishment from the globes
of my breasts in pearly white gulps,

your thighs creasing and bucking,
uncertain as a foal – I was nothing
but a larder preserving your nectar

in these domes of hips, milk pooling
at my waist. Now, in the night's dull
heat you stir, reach for the bottle,

find comfort in its rubber tip. Milk spills,
bone white, from my chest, rolls
a tearful pearl along my clavicle.

Snow Day on the Graig

The snow brings it back in slow indigo
        the terraced houses crystallised
        like teeth in the mountainside,
the way the Graig became a sheepskin rug,
and the globe of him, his arctic curves,

waist kneaded by tiny knuckles, head
rolled round as a thistle. He was pressed
powder, flecked with gravel and dirt, formed
of that hard-packed snow fanging
our fingertips pink as hot little tongues.

He was pulped impermanence, seeping
felt-tip fibres, his grin inane – a wide jab
of dirty rocks slashing his milk-white face,
the neighbours' scarf trailing his belly
like a long, woollen umbilical.

I begged him to stay, that frigid visitor.
I wanted to lead him inside, to press
his numbing hands, shapeless as clay,
to my mother's swollen cheekbone,

to push back the bruise blooming there
like a knot of blackberries, to touch
his cool palm, gentle as snowfall,
to the pulsing imprint
of my father's fist.

Cofiwch Dryweryn

It came roaring   guzzling   hedgerows and birdsong
swallowing dinner tables whole
a dŵr ym mhobman   a dim byd ar ôl ond dagrau
it drowned the imprint of a hunched lady's
tattered shoes lugging stones   back and forth
from chapel   hoping to pocket some semblance
of her God   *Duw a ŵyr*   they flooded window panes
quelled gravestones   seeped their thirst into thighbones
and pearl earrings   snatched the tulips from our hands
and still they are not   quenched

Ffynnon Elian

They plough through underbrush and shrub,
snagging calves like meat-slabs on nettles, arrive
blackberry-bruised and worn as dogs, half-moons
verging opaline eyes, leathery soles threadbare
and spun loose. Pupils wide as caves,

they ask for: crops dry as cracked earth, fevers hot
as seabed fissures, the squat crouch of night pressing low
on the chest. These cardamom hands don't come cheap,
whittling magic like a priestess – half a crown
for the slow scratch of initials on crow-black slate
or jagged stone, a slip of silver for a whispered verse
at the well's waiting lip, the boulders shedding

like bone dust. Others offer sagging foxgloves, a hunk of bread
for the douse of clean water at their temples, a stinging
plunge into the still black bathing pool. They dribble coins
like treacle, mirrored stars hooking each grimy piece, whirling
like hagfish at the   collision of   copper   and   unholy water.

Jac

Your brother careens
like a shockwave. A sudden
pine needle jabbing inside,
insistent as a spaniel.
And you, still so small
but thigh-strong. Certain.
I watch you towering
wooden blocks, searching
only for the thrill of seeing
your creation teeter
like an unruly flagpole,
come clanging down
in a kaleidoscope of colour.
You laugh, and without hesitation,
        rebuild.

The Womb Speaks

Let's pretend, if you like, that it was always about the children,
their half-formed hearts, their muted cries. Say it again. Write it
on your placards: *we hear you.* His careless pen inks his name
like a God's, seals my fate in black and white.

The truth is this – I was sculpted to grow, stretching round
as a pumpkin. To carry life like two palms cupping water.
To purge it with a seismic surge. To do it again and again.

I know what you fear – the notion of me empty. Unwilling.
Scrunched as a fist and poised to strike, a snake coiled to a sizzle.
Picture my worth now in nine-month cycles, watch me billow
and bloom. Watch me swell like a red hot wound at his command.

Believe me –
I will wear these scars like jewels, mined hot from the earth.
I will bleed and leak. You shackle what you fear: the minotaur
pacing its maze. The circus bear sweating rags behind bars.
This vacant womb. Its deafening power.

Notes

The quote from Zelda Fitzgerald was published in Nancy Milford's 1970 biography, *Zelda*, and is drawn from a fragment of an unpublished story, 'The Big Top.'

The quote from Margaret Atwood appeared in an article entitled '"Enforced childbirth is slavery": Margaret Atwood on the right to abortion' published by *The Guardian* in May 2022, following the leaked Supreme Court draft regarding the overturning of the Roe vs Wade ruling.

The essay 'A Nation Divided on Abortion' by Zoë Brigley, which was mentioned in the Foreword to this collection, was first published in US Election Analysis by The Centre for Comparative Politics and Media Research in 2020.

Flash: quotes Sue Lawley interviewing Christine Keeler in 1989, (*Wogan*, BBC, 1989.) 'Peter,' 'Lovesick' and 'Escape' paraphrase Keeler's words from her autobiography, *The Truth at Last*, (Sidgwick and Jackson, 2001).

On Walking in the Rain: references Llanon slangs, which are narrow strips of farmland historically managed by single households which now surround the coastal walking paths.

Sometimes we Sit in the Car: This poem takes its name from Natalie Ann Holborow's 'Sometimes you Cry in this Car,' (published in *Small*, Parthian, 2021).

Poem for Marshae Jones: In 2019, Marshae Jones was indicted for manslaughter for losing a pregnancy after being shot in the abdomen. Her shooter remains free.

A Woman Born in Flame: This poem was written after Christina Thatcher's poem, 'Earth Witch,' (published in *Okay Donkey*, 2021)

Poem for Sarah Everard: While walking home at night, Sarah Everard was kidnapped, raped and murdered by a serving police officer in 2021. While her case received widespread media coverage, this abuse of power and authority by serving officers is not a one-off. Between 2017 and 2021, nearly 2,000 police officers, special constables and PCSOs in the UK were accused of some form of sexual misconduct. [Source: *Channel 4 Dispatches Cops on Trial*, 11th October 2021]

Letter from Zelda Fitzgerald: paraphrases words taken from the letters exchanged between Zelda Fitzgerald and her husband, F. Scott Fitzgerald.

Blessing for the Women: In spring 2022, a leaked Supreme Court draft opinion suggested the court could be poised to overturn Roe v. Wade, leaving the legal status of abortion entirely up to individual states, compromising millions of women's lives and putting their bodies under the governance of others.

Woman and Child, Qinghai: This poem was written in response to a photograph of the skeletal remains of a woman and child unearthed in the Lajia site in the Qinghai province of China.

Cofiwch Dryweryn:

a dŵr ym mhobman	and water everywhere
a dim byd ar ôl ond dagrau	and nothing left but tears
Duw a ŵyr	God knows

Fynnon Elian: The holy well of St Elian became known from the end of the 18th century as 'the Cursing Well' with reports of the malice and evil that was said to take place there reaching as far overseas as South Asia. It was said that people had died as a direct result of being cursed at Ffynnon Elian, or had lived out their lives in fear and dread.

The Womb Speaks: references The Global Gag Rule. In January 2017, the then newly appointed US administration re-introduced a Republican policy that blocked Government funding to non-US organisations that perform abortion with their own funding. Since its introduction, The Global Gag Rule has put millions of women's lives at risk.

Acknowledgements

Several poems from this collection were first published in journals and anthologies including *Poetry Wales, New Welsh Reader, Black Bough: Deep Time, Well, Dam!* and *The Greek Anthology of Young Welsh Poets.*

'A Sudden Mother: (Staying on the Postnatal Ward During Covid-19)' won second place in the Sylvia Plath Poetry Prize and was published in the subsequent Nine Arches Press anthology, *After Sylvia.* 'Eve' received a special mention for the 2020 Poetry London Prize.

I would like to thank the team at Parthian, particularly Susie Wildsmith, for her astute editing of this collection. I must also mention my friends and colleagues Dr Emma Butler-Way, who never tired of offering her opinion when asked, and Alex Hubbard, whose constant encouragement has been much appreciated.

I must also, as always, thank The Salty Poets – Emily Vanderploeg, Rae Howells, Natalie Ann Holborow, Rhys Owain Williams, Adam Silman and Al Kellerman – who have been endlessly patient, supportive and kind.

I am grateful to Fionn Wilson for permission to use her painting, 'Christine Keeler Mesmerises' on the cover of this book.

With thanks also to Seymour Platt for permission to reprint images of his mother, Christine Keeler, photographed by Lewis Morley in 1963.

For more information on Christine Keeler, including the groundbreaking campaign for her pardon, see Platt's website:

www.christine-keeler.co.uk/campaign.html

Finally, I must thank Llewelyn, as well as his as-yet unborn brother, whom we are expecting shortly. Thank you both for choosing me to be your mother, and for trusting me in this chaotic and remarkable role. I won't always get it right, but I will always love you, protect you, and raise you with kindness, empathy and compassion. *Cofiwch – mor fawr a'r byd.*

PARTHIAN *Poetry*

Windfalls
Susie Wild
ISBN 978-1-912681-75-4
£9 | Paperback

'Wild comes across as the poetic equivalent of Jean Rhys: wry, arch, a little world-weary but, unlike Rhys, with a sparkling glint of humour... A very affecting collection of poems indeed.'
– Buzz Magazine

Small
Natalie Ann Holborow
ISBN 978-1-912681-76-1
£9 | Paperback

'Shoot for the moon? Holborow has landed, roamed its face, dipped into the craters, and gathered an armful of stars while up there.'
– Wales Arts Review

The language of bees
Rae Howells
ISBN 978-1-913640-69-9
£9 | Paperback

'rich in love, for the world that we are inseparable from and on the verge of destroying.'
– Matthew Francis

PARTHIAN *Poetry*

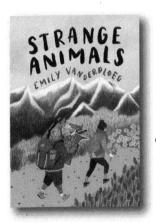

Strange Animals
Emily Vanderploeg
ISBN 978-1-913640-70-5
£9 | Paperback

'Emily Vanderploeg's clear-eyed lyric poetry explores the questions of where we belong, who we have become, and who or what undertakes that journey alongside us.'
– **Carolyn Smart**

How to Carry Fire
Christina Thatcher
ISBN 978-1-912681-48-8
£9 | Paperback

'A dazzling array of poems both remarkable in their ingenuity, and raw, unforgettable honesty.'
– **Helen Calcutt**

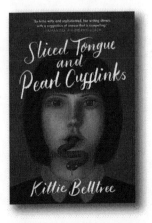

Sliced Tongue and Pearl Cufflinks
Kittie Belltree
ISBN 978-1-912681-14-3
£9 | Paperback

'By turns witty and sophisticated, her writing shivers with a suggestion of unease that is compelling.'
– **Samantha Wynne-Rhydderch**

PARTHIAN *Poetry*

Hymnal
Julia Bell

ISBN 978-1-914595-11-0
£9 | Paperback

'Moving, tender writing with a haunting
evocation of place and time.'
– Hannah Lowe

Visiting Aberaeron in the 1960s, Bell's
father heard a voice directing him to
minister to the Welsh. This unique
memoir in verse tells a story of religion,
sexuality, and family.

Moon Jellyfish Can Barely Swim
Ness Owen

ISBN 978-1-913640-97-2
£9 | Paperback

'Form and feeling combine to create a collection
which rewards the reader with a mesmerising
portrait of a much-loved landscape brimming
with startling imagery.'
– Samantha Wynne-Rhydderch

Moon jellyfish live a life adrift. Owen's
second collection explores what it is to
subsist with whatever the tides bring.
Poems that journey from family to
politics, womanhood and language.